SCHIRMER'S LIBRARY
OF MUSICAL CLASSICS

Vol. 1532

M. CLEMENTI

Two Sonatas

For Two Pianos, Four Hands

Edited by

EDWIN HUGHES

ISBN 0-7935-5206-0

G. SCHIRMER, Inc.

DISTRIBUTED BY

HAL•LEONARD®

Sonata I

Edited by Edwin Hughes

M. Clementi

Sonata II

Edited by Edwin Hughes

M. Clementi